There's A Drum In My Head

*To Frank Armitage, whose beautiful vision
has taught me so much*

Copyright © 1987 by Janice Schwegler
Published by Price/Stern/Sloan Publishers, Inc.
360 North La Cienega Boulevard, Los Angeles, California 90048

ISBN 0-8431-1982-9

There's A Drum In My Head

by
Janice
Schwegler

PRICE/STERN/SLOAN
Publishers, Inc., Los Angeles

There are sounds in the air everywhere.
And a special part of me
   that I always have around
   lets me hear.

There's a drum inside my head,
   in my ear.
And every sound I hear makes
   a wave in the air
   that hits the drum.

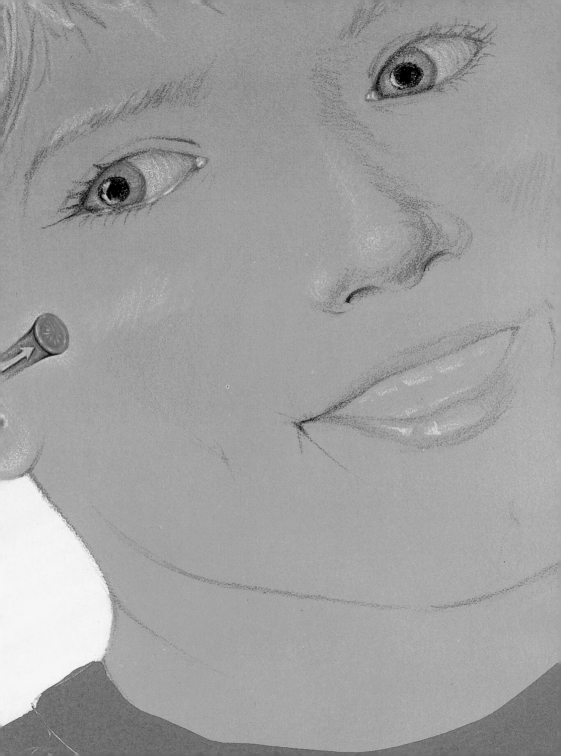

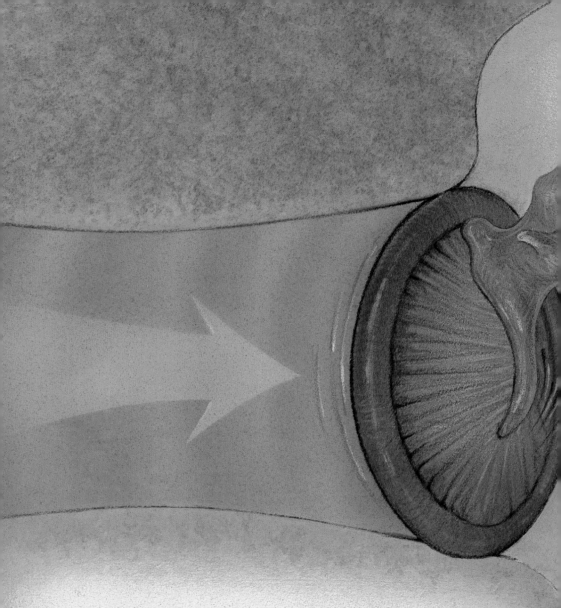

There are three tiny bones beside the drum.
Every movement in the drum is picked up
by the bones so they move, too.

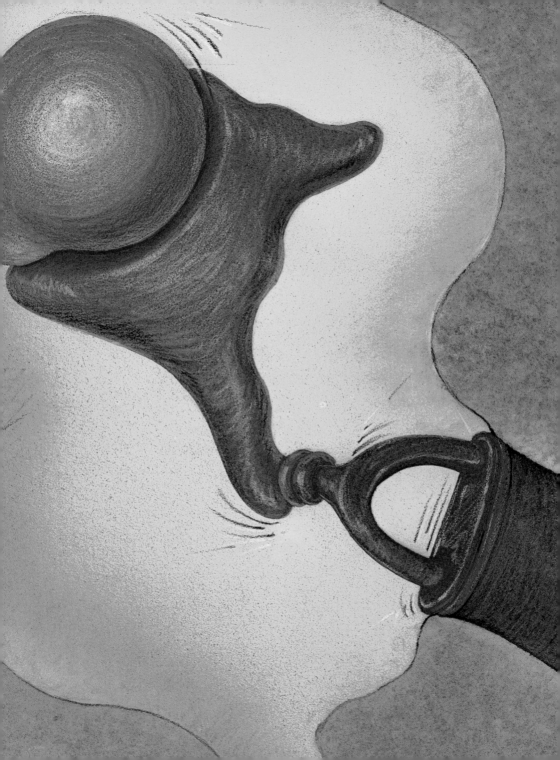

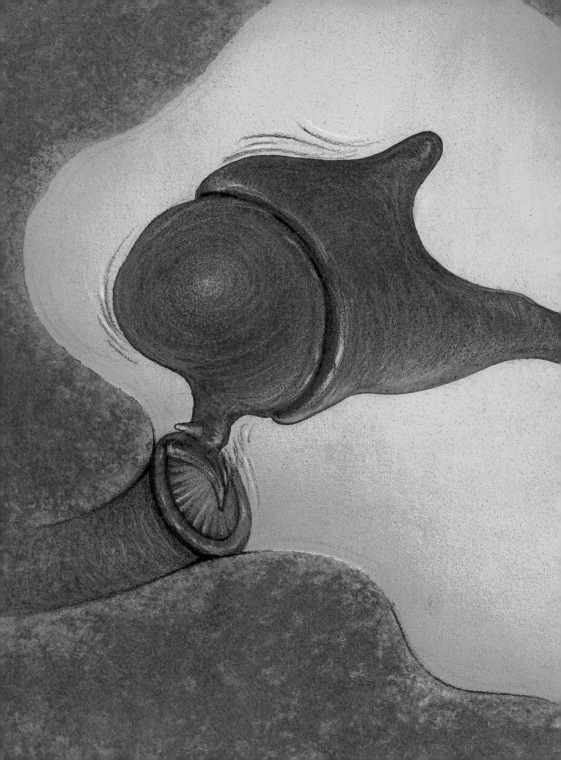

There's a window near the bones,
   oval-shaped.
And each movement in the bones
   presses on the window pane
   and it moves, too.

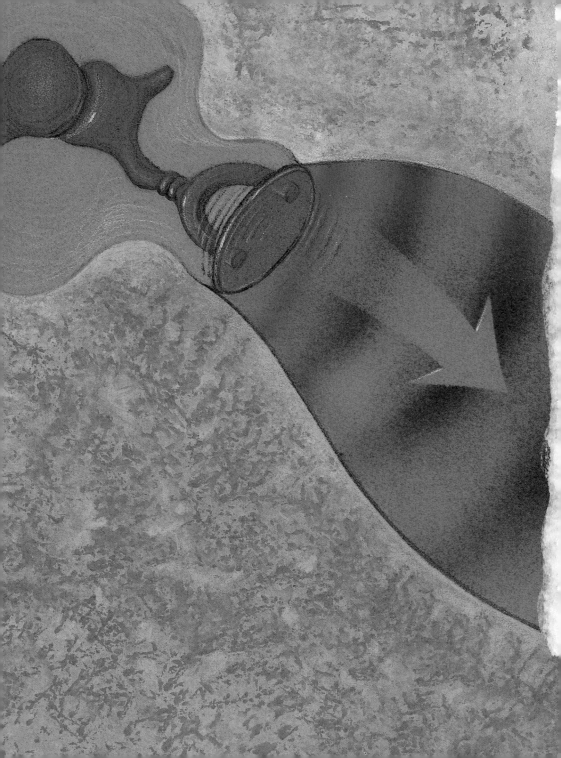

There is water by the window, in a tube.
Every time the window moves, it makes
a wave across the water in the tube.

The tube becomes a shell,
  inside my ear.
Waves of water in the tube
  travel deep inside the shell
  and go around.

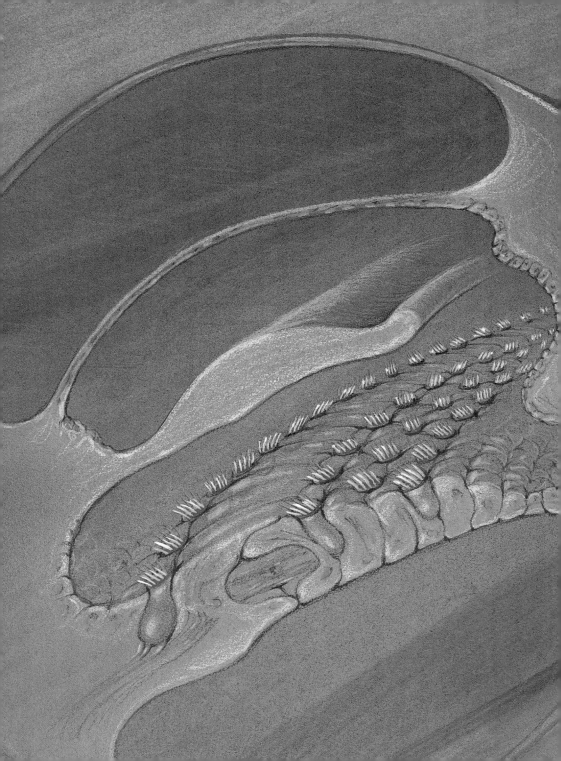

There are hairs in the shell in pretty rows.
When the wave comes in it hits so gently
that each hair sways back and forth.

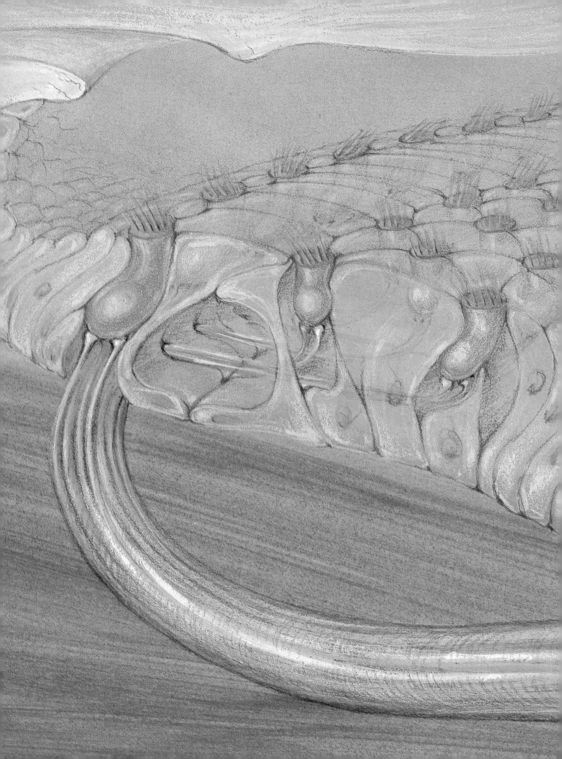

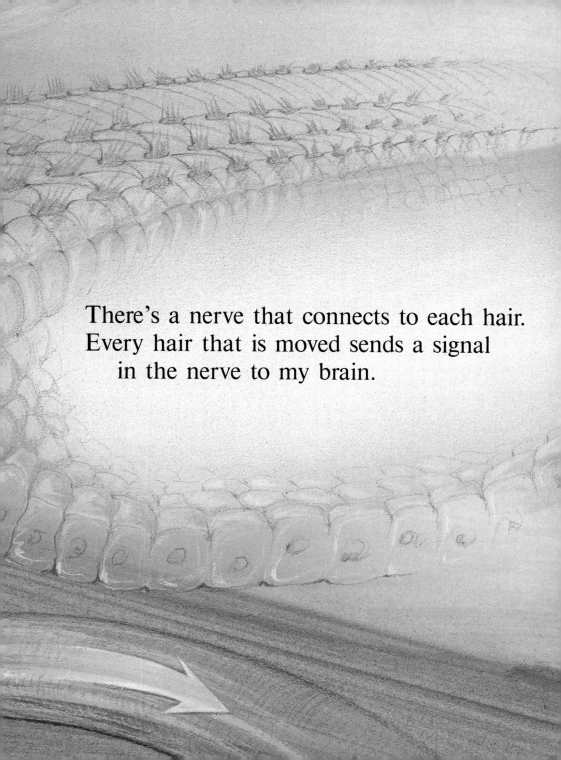

There's a nerve that connects to each hair.
Every hair that is moved sends a signal
in the nerve to my brain.

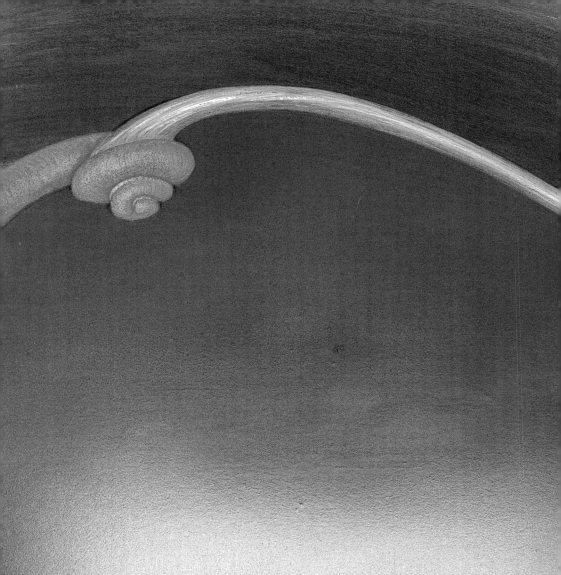

There's a place in my brain just for sounds.
When the signal arrives in my brain
I know that I hear.

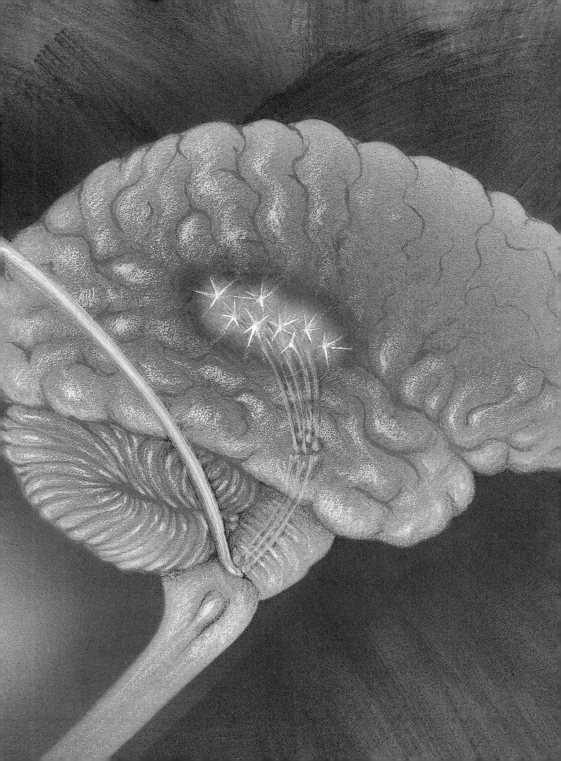

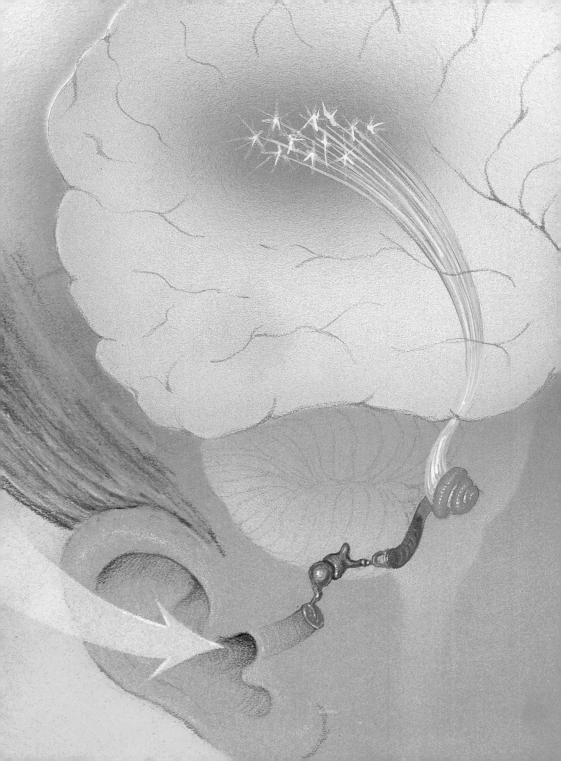

So, the sounds in the air hit the drum
    to move the bones and the window
    and start a little wave.

The wave goes down the tube to the shell,
    to make the rows of moving hairs
    send a signal in the nerve.

Right to my brain.